GET OUT OF YOUR THINKING BOX

365 Ways to Brighten Your Life
&
Enhance Your Creativity

by

Lindsay Collier

Robert D. Reed, Publishers
San Francisco, California

Robert D. Reed, Publishers

750 La Playa, Suite 647 • San Francisco, CA 94121
Telephone: 1-800-774-7336 • Fax: 408-255-8830

Editing & Back Cover by Pamela D. Jacobs, M.A.
Cover & Inside Illustrations by Timothy J. Strickling
Layout & Typesetting by Joseph E. Haga
Author's Photo by Leichtner Studios, New York

Library of Congress Cataloging-in-Publication Data
Collier, Lindsay.
    Get out of your thinking box : 365 ways to brighten your life & enhance your creativity / Lindsay Collier.
        p.   cm.
    ISBN 1-885003-01-3 : $7.95
    1. Creative ability in business.   2. Creative thinking.
  I. Title.
  HD53.C65   1994
  650. 1—dc20
                                        94-17657
                                        CIP

Designed, typeset, and manufactured in the United States of America.

Dedication

To Jan—my wife and friend for more than 32 years.

To Joe — Best of
luck to you —

Finley C.

Enjoy !

Acknowledgments

My thanks to those who have encouraged me to create this book, especially my children, Stephen, Gregory, and Laurel—who also contributed some great suggestions.

Special thanks to Robert Reed (my publisher), to Pamela Jacobs (editor), to Joe Haga (publication designer/typesetter), and Tim Strickling (artist) for their support and expertise in the production of this book.

Preface

I have spent over 25 years studying how to create the capability within our work places to use the creative capacity of people. I've tried literally hundreds of different idea stimulating techniques with people at all levels in business, sometimes with remarkable results and sometimes with marginal results. Those that were not as successful usually just failed to get people to make significant shifts in their thinking.

Today some wonderful techniques are available to help people expand their thinking; however, they all depend on our ability to accept a different framework of possibilities. It is easy for us to get locked into thinking along fairly narrow lines. This book is meant to be a lot of fun but it also is meant to help you get beyond your normal way of viewing things.

I hope that you enjoy the book and that it creates some valuable thinking shifts for you. If there are some particular things that you do to get out of your own thinking box I'd love to hear about them. You can reach me by telephone at 716-334-4779 or fax 716-359-9744. Or write to me at P.O. Box 352, West Henrietta, New York 14586.

Introduction

Why do we need to get out of our thinking boxes and what is a thinking box anyway? You may ask—why on earth should I hand over my hard earned money to read this silly sounding book? Because it may help you to create some tremendous breakthroughs in whatever you are doing. And you may have a very enjoyable time while doing it!

We all observe our world through a fairly intricate set of filters, helping us to some extent make sense of everything. Unfortunately these filters can block us from seeing our hidden potential or opportunities. There is a lot more space outside a box than there is inside. Many of us are actually quite comfortable in these boxes. It's warm and cozy, and we don't run the risk of making any mistakes. So we will look good most of the time. It's also pretty dull in there. If you are expected to be creative now and then, this won't happen from inside a box. For some people, getting out of their box is a major undertaking. You may have to stick your hand or foot out for a test. Then begin taking small trips, being careful not to stray too far in case you need to get back in real quick. As you become more familiar with the territory outside you can stray farther and farther away. Eventually, you may not need to go back into the box at all. But, be careful. Once outside the box, there is a fairly strong force pushing you back inside or pulling you to build a new box.

The following are some trips you can take when you are stuck in your thinking and need a small (or, perhaps large) mind quake. They involve "thinking something different", "being someone different", or "doing something different". Actually, you don't have to wait until you are stuck, especially since most of us will never admit that we're stuck.

No matter what you're doing, there is always some space to view your situation differently. When you leave your box, don't act as if it is your first walk on the moon. Enjoy it and learn a valuable way of enhancing your ability to bring some of your wonderful (possibly latent) creative thoughts into anything you are doing.

If you are a part of a group that could use some different thinking then pick a few suggestions that you may try as a group. It is important to stay loose and to ask yourself after each of these trips, "What did I learn?".

Here goes... have fun!

1. Complete the question, "Wouldn't it be ridiculous if _____?", as many ways as you can. Then find as many ways as you can to make these ridiculous things happen.

2. Walk backwards up a hill or, if you can't find a hill, just spend some time walking backwards.

3. Read some poetry or fairy tales and find some connections to what you are currently involved in.

4. Order a strange flavor of ice cream (sword fish, sardine, etc.) at an ice cream shop.

5. Find someone you never met and reminisce with them.

6. Have a good whining session with someone. Do it in a mall or restaurant for maximum benefit.

7. Talk in a nonsense language and pretend you really know what you are talking about.

8. Wear a clown nose or Groucho disguise while driving, or wear one of them at your office.

9. Read the paper upside down and see how much of it makes sense or what different messages you get. It may be interesting to see if anyone notices.

10. Ride your bicycle through a fast food restaurant's drive-through service.

11. Pay the toll for the car behind you at a toll booth.

12. Walk around in stilts for a while or strap some blocks to your shoes. Carefully note the differences in what you see.

13. Whittle a piece of wood.

14. Pollinate some flowers, using a cotton swab or something. Make sure there are no union bees watching you.

15. Flash a big smile to the person in the car next to you at a traffic light. Why not smile at everyone you see today?

16. Beat your PC with a whiffle bat or throw nerf darts at it.

17. Dress up like Wayne Newton and go to a Karaoke club. My guess is that many of you will skip over this one.

18. Call a few numbers at random and say, "I just want to wish you a nice day".

19. Drive to work using a totally different route.

20. Rather than speaking to each other at the next meeting, sing to each other in a light opera style.

21. Have a "whine and jeez" party at work to get it all out of your system.

22. Design a logo that represents what your major strength is and a slogan that says what you are all about.

23. Dress up your dog or cat.

24. Carry a silly grin on your face for a whole day (or at least during the entire trip to work).

25. Wander around a toy store. Buy a toy for yourself.

26.

Practice "reflective listening" by mirroring the conversations you have with people. Reflect, without judgment, back to them what they are saying to you.

27. Stop at a car service station and ask to have the air changed in your tires.

28. Go to a bank and ask for change for a nickel.

29. Go to a Burger King and order a Big Mac and a Frosty.

30. Fax some of your favorite cartoons to your friends.

31. Pick two unrelated things out of a catalog and see how many creative combinations you can make of them.

32. Spend an evening reading children's books.

33. Get a massage or give one to someone you like.

34. Sit down and do some drawing. Try to draw the space around an object rather than the object.

35. Concentrate on thinking about thinking. Jot down all the things that come to mind as you do this. Identify ways you might change the way you think.

36. Visit a sick friend or relative and cheer them up.

37. Listen to tapes of old radio shows (Charley McCarthy, Jack Benny, Amos & Andy).

38. Rent the strangest sounding video you can find at a video store.

39. Pretend to be your favorite celebrity and look at things through his or her eyes for a day.

40. Get a coloring book and pretend you're a kid again.

41. Think of yourself as your favorite comedian for the day.

42. Read a science fiction book or write a short science fiction story related to something that is currently important to you.

43. Make paper airplanes or paper dolls.

44. Go to a coffee shop and sniff all of the coffee beans.

45. Think of yourself as a certain animal all day. What is your new perspective? How do you feel? What adventures do you take?

46. Take a drive to a place you never go.

47. Read the jackets of your record and compact disc collection.

48. Study a flower or a leaf very carefully. What are the similarities between it and your current situation?

49. Think of all the ways that your job is like a Slinky.

M ore than any time in history, mankind faces a crossroads. One path leads to despair and utter hopelessness, the other to total extinction. Let us pray that we have the wisdom to choose correctly.

-Woody Allen

50. Write a song.

51. Try a different food combination, one that is really different (mustard on watermelon, hot dogs with peanut butter and jelly).

52. Make friends with a homeless person. Take him or her out to dinner if you can.

53. Think of something important in your life or work. Identify some organisms that would seem to be a good metaphor. Sit down and draw a picture of this and enhance it any way that comes to mind. What different thoughts come from this?

54. Go skip rocks on a pond.

55. Pick up some trash along the street.

56. Sleep on the opposite side of the bed or face the opposite direction.

57. Write and mail a letter to yourself. Tell yourself all the nice things you can think of.

58. Look up 10 strange words in the dictionary and use them within the next few days.

59. Go test drive a new car. Don't skimp on this – you don't have to buy it. Or you may want to test out that 18 wheeler truck that you've always dreamed of.

60. Go to a small town and make some friends. Find out what is interesting and important to them.

61. Stand on a highway bridge and wave at people driving by.

62. Go bird watching.

63. Go for a walk someplace you've never been before, carefully observing everything around you. What did you see that was interesting?

64. Read a book of Indian folklore. How do these stories connect to your own situation? How do they help you to think differently?

65. Play solitaire.

66. Do absolutely nothing for a whole day. See how long you can go without thinking about anything. What was it like for you?

67. Write with your opposite hand or hold the pen between your toes.

If we think more about failing at what we are doing than about doing it, we will not succeed.

-Warren Bennis

68.

Ask yourself, "What would I do if I knew I could not fail?"

Things will get better—despite our efforts to improve them.

-Will Rogers

69. Put your shoes on the wrong feet and see how long it takes someone to notice. See how long it takes before you notice it.

70. Call others in the phone book with your same name and find out what you have in common with them. Ask their viewpoint on something that concerns you.

71. Write a letter of appreciation to someone who has helped you lately.

72. Take some pictures of flowers and other things in nature.

73. Pretend your head is a camera and shoot some pictures.

74. Read the introductory section of your phone book. You will be surprised at how interesting and informative it is.

75.

Smile all day long. Don't let the smile leave your face no matter what happens. You may want to reduce it to a smirk every now and then to rest your smile muscles. At the end of the day see how differently you feel.

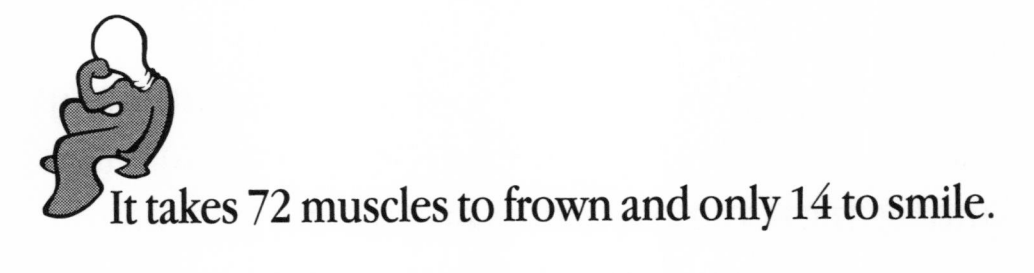
It takes 72 muscles to frown and only 14 to smile.

76. Wear a silly hat all day.

77. Walk a nature trail and find 5 analogies to your life and your work.

78. Take a trip on a map and try to experience it as though you are really there.

79. Wear polka dot underwear. You already are? Go on to the next one.

80. Pretend you are an electron flowing through a power line. What does it feel like? What do you see? What are some things that you'd like to see changed?

81. Look at things through a large magnifying glass or through binoculars. What do you see differently?

82. Identify a few interesting internal body organs and identify the similarities between them and your life or your organization.

83. Go through your old picture albums.

84. Pick an interesting house plant and examine it closely. In what ways is it like your work or personal situation?

85. Closely observe an active ant colony. What can you learn from ants? How is your company like an ant colony?

86. Get up at 4:00 a.m. and take a walk.

87. Read a good cartoon book. Select a few cartoons that have an interesting connection to your current situation.

88. Browse through a good book store, spending most of your time in unfamiliar sections.

89. Sign up for an adult education course in a topic totally unrelated to your normal interests. After completing the course, identify why it is not totally unrelated.

90. Find out how something works, choosing something that you have often wondered about.

91. Learn an interesting phrase (such as, "I love you") in five languages.

92. Study some cloud formations. What new thinking comes from connections to these?

93. Count the leaves on a tree.

94. Draw something using a landscape as a metaphor to describe its characteristics.

95. Get a book of Native American Indian myths and stories. Make it a point to read a few each week and learn from them.

96. Visit a nursing home or hospice and talk with some people there. Share your laughter, photographs, stories, music, or art.

97. Walk around and call things by incorrect names. For example, look at a door and call it a horse; see a picture and call it a cup.

98. Buy a few masks and wear them for a while. Act like the person the mask portrays.

99. Draw some silly pictures.

100.

Take something apart and examine how it works. How would you make it differently? What are some parallels to something you are currently working on?

101.

Exchange business cards with another person and become that person for a while.

I was tempted to stop this list at 100 before asking how it's going. But I decided that it would be more in keeping with the theme of this book to let you do 101. Be honest...are you just reading these suggestions? Or are you trying some of them?

If you are just reading them, you're not getting the full benefit or the potential for changing your thinking. So try to do more than just read them. If you can, integrate these ideas into the working process of groups with which you are associated.

*I'll check back with you a bit later...
remember, I'm watching.*

102. Study a map of the United States. Ask people from various locations how they might think differently about some key problems on which you are working.

103. List names of some common items (such as cars) and mix up their letters. For example, a Ford becomes a Dorf. See how this may change your vision of that item.

104. Spend half an hour watching the dumbest TV program that you can find (usually not too hard to find).

105. Record a new and creative outgoing message for your message machine.

106. Go to a public meeting and carefully observe what's going on (the school board, a zoning committee, etc.).

107. Send some greeting cards to a few people whom you've never met and wish them a great day.

108. Sit down and have a conversation with a plant, or sing to it if you like. You may want to be sure that no one is observing you.

109. Spend a whole day as "someone else". Concentrate on seeing the world through his or her eyes.

110. Leaf through the yellow pages. Select 2 or 3 businesses and find interesting combinations of them. For example, an attorney who delivers pizza along with legal advice.

111. Do a mind map of all your thoughts for one hour.

112. Pretend to be a visitor from another planet for the day, looking at things through his or her eyes.

113. Identify all of the stupid things you've done this week or month. Think about all the reasons that they weren't so stupid after all.

114. Think of asking a comedy group to do a satire on your company. Decide how they would portray it. This may give you something to work on.

115. Do a crossword puzzle.

116. Think of various things that you could do to get fired from your job. How can you prevent these situations from happening?

117. Concentrate on absolutely nothing for 5 minutes. Can you do it? Is it hard for you?

118.

Type all your friends' names into a computer and then spell check them. The results may surprise you and give your friends a few laughs. For example, a friend of mine had her name spell checked as "cheery hormones".

119. Find a new and innovative way to sit in a chair and read a book.

120. Spend some time trying to write backwards or upside down.

121. Climb a tree and spend some time observing the world from that standpoint.

122. Think about some common annoyances in life and make up some new words for them. What new ideas come from these words?

123. Think about what it would be like if some of the non-human things around you began to act human. For example, what if your oak tree had a blind date with your Bradford pear?

124. Visit an airport and watch what is happening without the worry of having to make a flight.

125.

Interview some people. Tell them that you are writing a book and that you'd like their opinion on a certain topic.

In the past few years, if you haven't discarded a major opinion or acquired a new one check your pulse—you may be dead.

126. Buy the most foolish software game you can find and try it out.

127. Listen carefully to the words of a song by an artist such as Harry Chapin or Van Morrison. What do they mean to you right now?

128. Make up 10 of the silliest questions you can and try to answer them. Or ask your peers (a peer can be defined as "a person who enters a revolving door behind you and comes out in front").

129. Spend a day thinking in terms of the metric system.

130. Make up some new words to describe some of the things you see happening around you.

131. Cook a very strange meal (for some people, like me, every meal would probably be strange).

132. Gives names to objects around you and carry out a personal conversation. For example, after naming your car "Bob" ask it, "So what's it like being a car, Bob?".

133. Spend the day being your favorite hero or heroine. Think as she or he would and try to act that way as well.

134. Read the dictionary.

135. Buy someone you love a present for no reason at all. Better still, buy someone you hate a present.

136. Play a game of catch with someone.

137. Pick up and read a newspaper from another state.

138. Shine your car and shine something in the engine compartment.

139. Read a science fiction magazine or, if you can't handle that, read MAD Magazine.

140. Write a short poem.

141. Watch a Star Trek episode.

142. Pick 2 unrelated products out of some magazine ads and see how many interesting combinations you can make with these.

143. Think about something terrible that is happening in your world right now. Ask yourself what is good about it. Use the results to think about what you can do to improve the situation.

144. Call two old friends that you have not talked with for years.

145. Listen to an opera, especially if you think you hate operas.

146. Listen to a radio talk show and try to agree with everything anyone says.

147. Find at least 2 reasons why everything <u>can</u> be done today.

148. Pretend you are a sponge for the day and soak up everything you hear. Later that evening, squeeze yourself out.

149. Listen to a Gregorian chant and let your mind flow free.

150. Spend 90% of your time in a meeting, listening carefully and trying to understand what others are saying from <u>their</u> point of view.

Everything should be made as simple as possible, but not simpler.

-Albert Einstein

The world we have made, as a result of the level of thinking done thus far, creates problems that we cannot solve at the same level at which we create them.

-Albert Einstein

151. Find a good picture of you as a child. Tape it to your bathroom mirror and use it every morning to bring out the "child" in you.

152. Smile the biggest smile you can and hold in for 5 minutes. Write down all the things that came to mind. Surprised?

153. Write all of the things that are keeping you from thinking outside the box on a roll of toilet paper...and then flush it.

154. Tap dance.

155. Retire to a quiet room by yourself and have a good belly laugh. You don't need anything funny since you will be your own entertainment. Look into a mirror if it helps.

156. Make up a "Rodney Dangerfield routine" about yourself. For example, I'm so smart that _____.

157. Write down all the values you have that drive your behavior.

158. Watch a good situation comedy on TV and just enjoy it.

159. Make up a science fiction story with you as the central character.

160. Wander around a college campus and visit their bookstore.

161. Clean some windows in your house—or someone else's house.

162. Pick up an *Utne Reader* and read it from cover to cover.

I t is only when we develop others that we permanently succeed.

-Harvey Firestone

163.

Spend the day focusing on giving everyone you talk to positive support in whatever they are doing.

164. Ask advice from a child.

165. Tinker around in your garage, cellar, or attic.

166. Talk to a turkey (a real one, I mean).

167. Go to one of those passport photo machines and take a picture of yourself making silly faces (thanks to C.W. Metcalf for this idea).

168. Build a musical instrument out of spare things around the house or office. You may want to have your entire group build an orchestra. Then you might as well write and play a symphony. Why stop now – record a CD!

169. Draw an item by drawing only the space around it. How is this thought transferred to your work?

170. Just let your mind wander around...and this time, follow it.

171. Read all of the want ads in your local newspaper.

172. Make up some new words. Send them to comedian, Rich Hall.

173. Spend the day thinking about yourself as your customer or client would. Jot down what you learn from this experience.

174. Write down all the happy words you can think of and then say them out loud to yourself or others.

175. Watch some Three Stooges videos.

176. Watch a Monty Python video.

177. Dress up in some out of style clothes. See if you can bring them back into style.

178. Rearrange the furniture in your office or a room in your house.

179. Have a monster garage sale. Think of it as cleaning out your mind as well as your house.

180. Explore some side streets downtown, or drive some rural roads that are really off the beaten path.

181. Dissect a piece of fruit (an orange, kiwi, etc.). Study the structure of it and compare it to your organization or your personal life.

182. Write a short story in phonetic language.

183. Listen to a very different radio show (like the polka hour).

184. Explore some yard sales.

Where there is an open mind, there will always be a frontier.

-*Charles Kettering*

185.

Brainstorm a very different list of job titles that you think you should have or would like to have.

186.

Make up some business cards for yourself, showing your occupation as "thinker", "person with brain", "nice guy", "caring person" or something similar.

187. Write all of the things that block your thinking or that bother you on pieces of paper. Put them in an old suitcase and stomp all over it. If you can't find an old suitcase, use a shredder or find another way to dispose of them.

188. Put a stamp on an old, dried up pancake. Write a note on it to a friend and send it to him or her through the mail. (Believe it or not, my daughter did this once and it made it through.)

189. Paint a room a unique color.

190. Cook a strange theme dinner (Northern Mexican Cajun Italian).

191. Color the pictures in a coloring book in the most wrong colors you can imagine.

192.

Spend an hour identifying your own unique ways to get out of your thinking rut. (If you like, write them down and send them to me for the next book. I'll be glad to give you credit for your ideas.)

193. For one day, take the perspective of the opposite sex.

194. Read a book on something you know nothing about and for which you have no particular interest.

195. Take black and white pictures.

196. Build a sand castle.

197. Try to talk as fast as you can.

198. Mow the lawn in a totally different pattern. (I mean *totally* different). Then, mow your neighbor's lawn.

199. Watch the film *Dead Poet's Society*. How many lessons are there on thinking outside your box?

200. Take a tour of your local TV news room.

201. Visit an art or science museum.

202. Collect some objects from nature and make something out of them (such as pussy willows, acorns, branches, etc.)

203. Document your day with a camcorder.

204. Jot down all of the strange clichés that you can think of. Play with them in your mind or act them out. For example, what does it mean to "Pull the wool over one's eyes"? Get some wool and pull it over your eyes to see what happens. Is it any different if you use cotton or a blend?

205. Go to a strange food section of your market. Buy something for yourself or something as a gift. Invent a new and strange food yourself (pickled black beans in watermelon sauce).

206. Go through some of your memorabilia.

207. Spend the day making creative combinations of things you see. One 10 year old girl combined a Christmas tree angel with a smoke detector to come out with a product called a "Guardian Angel".

208. Ask everyone you see today about some of their fantasies. What are some things that they wish they had, wish they could do, or wish was true? In what ways does this stimulate your thinking?

209. Concentrate for a while on trying to be dyslexic, reversing your letters and words. Find out how this changes your perspective.

210. If your current situation were a vehicle, what type would it be? Make a drawing of it.

211. Take a power snooze.

212. Think about all the things that are unique about you. In what ways might you capitalize on these unique characteristics?

213. Tell someone something about yourself that hardly anyone knows. Find out something similar about someone else.

214. Contact the author of a book you recently read and tell him/her how much you enjoyed it. Ask about their secrets to writing.

215. Concentrate on ideas you've never thought of before.

216. Visualize yourself in a time machine, projecting yourself forward and backward in time. How has thinking changed in these time periods?

*O*kay, time out again. I told you that I'd be watching and I've noticed how you tend to skip over the ones that seem too much of a stretch. Don't fear! Ask yourself—am I really serious about changing how I think or is this just fluff?

Why not go back and pick a few suggestions that are a substantial stretch for you and try them out. I think that you may be surprised. Or if you're one of those compulsive readers who must get to the end of a book before you take any action, highlight ideas that you want to try. I understand you because I tend to do things that way, too. The important thing is that you devote real time to "doing" rather than to "reading".

217. You have just read about the latest discovery that our world is all contained inside a large ball and it is painted bright blue inside. How does this concept change your thinking?

218. Find a quiet place and get into a "thinking position". Lean on a table with your hand supporting your chin and stare into space. Remain in that position until some new thoughts come to you.

219. Say at least two things good about everything you hear today.

220. Go to the supermarket and buy some of that strange fruit you've always seen and passed by.

221. Study a famous leader and think about the thing that made her or him successful.

222. Read a joke book.

223. Find a place where you can close your eyes and concentrate on the sounds and smells of the environment. What do you "see" that you didn't see with your eyes? (I suggest that you don't try this while driving your car.) Try this again, using ear plugs to block out the sounds around you.

224. Spend the day as a "spy" from your competition. Every time you do something make a note of it, as the spy would do.

225. Think about something that you or your company are doing and write down all the implications of it. For every implication look at the next level of implications; take this to several levels.

226. Take a familiar product and identify all of the ways in which it could be made simpler to use.

227. Take an idea or a problem that you have been thinking about lately. Generate as many totally outrageous solutions as you can think of. Then think about how you could make these outrageous solutions workable.

228. Spend half an hour doodling. What do your doodles tell you?

229. Pick a few familiar objects and become them in your mind. How does it feel? How does being that object change your thinking about it?

230. Switch projects temporarily with someone else. Each of you can write down as many ideas and thoughts as possible, without knowing too much about the other's project.

The winner sees a green near every sandtrap. The loser sees a sandtrap near every green.

Optimists see an opportunity in every problem. Pessimists see a problem in every opportunity.

Some people never hear opportunity knock because they are too busy knocking opportunity.

-Hal Chadwick

231. Pick an object, any object, and identify 50 things that you might do with it. When you've finished identify 50 more.

232. Think of as many nonsense words as you can. How do some of these words help you to think differently about something you are working on?

233. Get a book of clichés, proverbs, and maxims. Find some that help you shift your thinking about something that is important to you.

234. Go buy a Mr. Potato Head and use him to ask for different viewpoints. Set him at a place of honor in your next meeting and ask his opinion whenever your group is stuck for ideas.

235. Play a game of Scrabble, using a foreign language.

I don't want any "yes" men around me. I want people who will tell me the truth even if it means their job.

-Samuel Goldwyn

 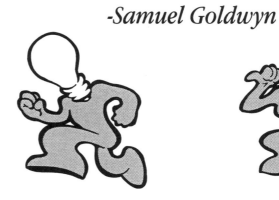 

237.

Give your boss some positive feedback or just ask her or him out for a friendly lunch.

No great idea ever entered the mind through the mouth.

238.

Ask for someone's opinion. Choose someone who has no knowledge of your particular problem, situation, or opportunity. Try asking a child, a person from an unrelated field, a senior citizen, or a visitor from abroad—or another planet.

239. Go to a park and write a short story or an article on a topic that interests you.

240. Cut out a bunch of interesting pictures from some magazines and make a collage. Use this as a springboard for new ideas.

241. Buy and read a book of local history.

242. Build a model plane or car.

243. Identify all the oxymorons that seem to fit your situation. (For those of you who are unfamiliar with these, oxymorons are two words that typically don't fit together—such as: Senate ethics, professional wrestling, or military intelligence.)

244. Look through some catalogs and find some interesting objects that relate to your current area of interest.

245. Try your best to draw something. If you're not satisfied with it, trick yourself by drawing the space around it or by drawing it upside down.

246. Visit a cemetery and read the epitaphs. What would you want on your epitaph?

247. Visit a craft shop and find a few items that seem to provide an interesting metaphor related to something of importance to you.

248. Have an "out of body" experience. (I'm not exactly sure what this is but it sounds interesting.)

249. Talk to your subconscious as a friend. Ask it to solve a problem for you just before you go to sleep.

250.

Exaggerate everything you think about today.

Get your facts first, and then you can distort them as much as you please.

-Mark Twain

251. Invent the "walk" of your organization, one that clearly depicts the characteristics of it. If you are not associated with an organization, invent one that shows how you feel right now and one that represents how you want to feel.

252. Create a personal logo for yourself and a few slogans that seem to say what you are all about.

253. Concentrate on something that you've never thought of before.

254. Invent a perpetual motion machine.

255. Go to an arcade and play as many of the machines as you can. In what ways does each of these represent a good analogy to something you are working on?

256. Concentrate on floating like a cloud. What do you see? How do you feel? How high up are you?

257. Refinish an old piece of furniture.

258. Sleep in a different room tonight.

259. Buy a book of brain-teasers and challenge yourself.

260. Listen to a great symphony, focusing only on the music and any visualizations it may produce. Beethoven's Sixth Symphony (Pastoral) is a great starting point.

261. Make up some new words and then invent the products that these words might describe.

262. Take a nice, long hot bath. Don't forget to bring a rubber duck.

263.

Think of all the ways that you could really mess up today. Go all out to identify mistakes that you could make. Focus on making these as terrible as possible. What good could possibly come from these mistakes?

To create you must first destroy.

-Picasso

264. Find yourself a great "thinking hat" and put it on any time that you want to think differently.

265. Search for a plant with a unique structure to help you describe, in rather different terms, something that you are working on currently. For example, how would a spider plant suggest different ways to structure a project team?

266. Search through all of your computer screen saver alternatives.

267. Go antique shopping.

268. Visit your City Hall and look up some of the new business names. See what new opportunities might appeal to you.

269. Rearrange your office and purge your files.

270. Make a list of all the things that you would do if only you had the time.

271. Spend some time defining what you want to create in your life or work. Focus on closing the gap between where you are right now and where you want to be. How does your thinking change?

272. Go to an amusement park and take some rides.

273. Listen to some "high energy" music.

274. Do a mind map of all your thoughts at the present moment.

275. Sit outside on a warm summer night and watch the stars. Think of the space between the stars as places from which new ideas emerge.

Two roads diverged in the wood, and I took the one less traveled by, and that has made all the difference.

-Robert Frost

276.

Concentrate on thinking about everything nobody else is thinking, or going where nobody else is going.

277.

Have a serious conversation with your dog or cat.

Don't accept your dog's admiration as conclusive evidence that you are wonderful.

-Ann Landers

278. Visit the ocean. Watch the waves and listen to the sound.

279. Think of your self as being in a really strange place (inside your computer, on the moon, in the binding of a book, etc.) How does it feel there? And what different viewpoints do you get?

280. Go to a crowded, busy, noisy place where nobody knows you or expects anything from you.

281. Watch cartoons for a while.

282. Do some aerobic exercise or get on an exercise machine. The more often, the better.

283. Go fly a kite.

284. Have a few drinks and work on developing new ideas for your problem or opportunity. (Supposedly, this was a favorite technique of the Persians but I don't suggest you do this often.)

285. Do some sculpturing with clay or another more aggressive material.

286. Build a house of cards.

287. Go swimming or sit in a steam bath, sauna, or Jacuzzi.

288. Play a game.

289. Read a book of myths and identify the meanings they have for you and your work.

290. Go to a trade show, particularly one outside your own trade.

291.

Spend some time concentrating on using different senses than you would normally. For example, try smelling or visualizing music as well as listening to it. If you are captivated by the smells of your favorite restaurant, try listening to the sounds and focusing on the feelings of it.

See what you can hear. Hear what you can touch. Feel what you can smell. Smell what you can see.

292. Think of yourself as being various internal body organs. How does it feel to be a stomach? What are some things that bother you? What are some things that you like about the job? How is being a stomach much like your current situation?

293. Make a conscious effort to do everything in a distinctly opposite way. Shake hands with people with your left hand. Put your underpants on backwards. For everything you do, find what is opposite and do it that way. Be sure to use some discretion. For example, don't drive on the opposite side of the road.

294. Make a list of the most stupid questions that you can think of.

295. Think up as many things as you can that have never been invented.

296. Draw a picture of all the emotions you are feeling right now.

297. Browse through the reference section of the library. Find at least 10 interesting things that you didn't know before.

298. Make up 10 really foolish statements. List reasons why they aren't as foolish as you originally thought. For example, "If I could fit the moon into my dishwasher I'm sure that our potatoes would be spicier".

299. Make 2 columns of random words and select a few word pairs by taking one from each column. How do these word pairs change your thinking?

300. Select some of your favorite cartoons and invent new punch lines for them.

301. Think of all the words that rhyme with a key word that expresses how you feel right now. Select a few that seem to be interesting springboards for some different thinking.

302. Search out 10 different objects and construct something interesting and useful out of them.

303. What are some key words that relate to your work? For each of them identify some different words to use. How does this make you think differently about them?

304. Write all of your excuses for not accomplishing things on small scraps of paper. Visualize them inside a balloon which floats away in the wind.

No snowflake in an avalanche

feels responsible.

305. Select a few names randomly from the phone book and write a story about them. What would these new characters think about some of the things that are currently important to you?

306. Draw your thinking box. What is inside? What is outside?

307. Get a book of good quotations and select a few interesting ones that seem to apply to the thinking shifts you are looking for.

308. Read *All the Thinks You Can Think* by Dr. Seuss.

309. Identify all of the "sacred cows" associated with your work or personal life. Determine how you can slay those cows. When you're done, celebrate by taking your significant other out for a hamburger.

310. Reframe you problem or situation. Create a picture of it, zoom in, change the brightness and sharpness knob, and speed up and slow down the movement. Look at it through a wide angle lens, and make any other adjustments that you can think of.

311. Take your dog for a long walk. If you don't have a dog, borrow your neighbor's dog. Or take someone you like for a walk.

312. Look for the "rightness" in every thought or idea that comes to you today. Concentrate on finding no wrong in anything.

313. Go to the newsstand and find several magazines which are different from those you would usually buy. Find some interesting connections between the content of these and what you are currently working on.

314. Identify as many analogies from nature as you can. Select a few to help you think differently about your current opportunities.

315. Wander through a hardware store and find as many items as you can that may trigger new thoughts for you.

316. Ask yourself "why" (repeatedly) in regard to something you want to do or a problem you want to solve. How does your thinking change when you reach a point where you've run out of answers?

Be what you is, not what you ain't—cause if you is what you ain't, you ain't what you is.

-Luther D. Price,

jazz musician

317. Think about who your customers are at the present time and put yourself in their shoes.

318. If there were a book or movie written about your life or your organization what would it be? Play with this one for a while, come up with several titles, and select one that suggests some very different thinking.

319. Read a science fiction book or watch a science fiction video. Make connections to your present situation.

320. Think about the funniest thing that ever happened to you and laugh as loudly, as long, and as heartily as you possibly can about it. Laughter helps to change your perspective on things by opening up the mind for all sorts of new thoughts. If you can't think of anything funny just laugh anyway.

321.

Identify at least ten things that you could do to get a promotion. Could any of these really work?

Only those who risk going too far can know how far one can go.

-T.S. Eliot

322. Drop an imaginary bomb on whatever you are doing. Start from scratch with a new design. Pretend that the rules blew up along with everything else.

323. Skip through a mall or down the street. If you aren't ready to skip in public then skip around your house.

324. View everything as if you had eyes placed on your kneecaps.

325. Dental floss your teeth and think about how it would be if you could floss your mind. How would this flossing help you to think differently?

326. Wash a few windows in your house. As you clean each pane, see yourself removing a film of dirt which was clouding your vision of a clear future. What can you see better now?

327. Have lunch with a friend or an associate. Make it a point to fill up three napkins with new thoughts. Ideas that originate on napkins are usually the best ones.

328. Find a new and innovative position for thinking. You may want to lie on the floor with your feet up on a chair, stand on your head, or lean on your desk. Assume this position whenever you want to think differently.

329. Make up some jokes about your present situation.

330. Spend a whole day listening to the person inside you. Every time a word or interesting thought pops into your mind write it down. At the end of the day, brainstorm how each of these words or thoughts suggests a new idea related to your work.

331. Think of a common household item (such as a clock) and think up some of the most outrageous designs possible. Why aren't they so outrageous after all? How can you use these ideas for you own projects?

332. Spend some time viewing the world from an insect's perspective.

333. Give your brain a name (i.e., Bob) and try to form a friendly supportive relationship with it. When you need some different thinking, ask Bob.

334. Eavesdrop on some conversation. After listening to these people, what do you think they would say about some things that are important to you?

335.

Think of 10 things that are impossible for you to do that could drastically change your life or your organization. How could you make these happen?

You can keep the organization vital by not taking the organization too seriously.

-3M CEO

336.

Buy a Tonka dump truck and fill it with ideas. Place it on the conference table at your next meeting. Have people write down their ideas on index cards and put them in the truck. Take a few minutes at the end of meeting to check them out.

Anyone who can spell a word only one way is an idiot.

-W.C. Fields

337.

Pick a few interesting words and identify all of the ways that you can misspell them.

338. Think about all of the questions you have never asked.

339. Wander around in the reference section of your library. Find at least 10 interesting things that trigger some new thinking.

340. Carry out a few "man on the street" interviews.

341. Think of something that is important to you as if it were a three layer cake with icing. What are the layers and what is the icing?

342. Find as many common items as you can. Read the labels and the ingredients list. What thoughts come from this?

343. Take yourself on a guided imagery tour to a place in which you can think more expansively.

344. Sit down and read an article that you have randomly chosen from a magazine. What new thoughts are triggered by this?

345. Learn how to use the period of "reverie" (halfway between sleeping and waking) effectively. In the morning when you awake try to hold yourself in that reverie state. See how this gets you out of your normal thinking box.

346. Identify all new innovations you can think of. Write down all of the ideas you can "steal" from these.

347. Find the essence of some of the things that you are currently working on. For example, look back as far as possible to see how and where a problem began. Create a statement regarding your findings. See what new thinking opens up for you.

348.

Assemble a group that consists only of people who know nothing about what you do. Give them a brief update of some of your concerns and ask for their thoughts.

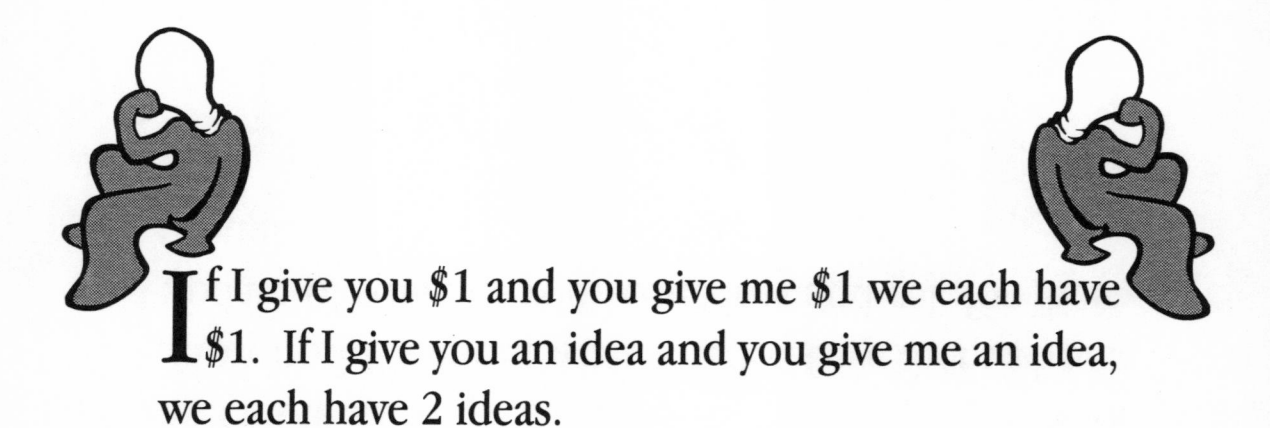

If I give you $1 and you give me $1 we each have $1. If I give you an idea and you give me an idea, we each have 2 ideas.

349.

Invent some new words to explain some interesting observations about your work. For example, what word would capture the tendency of managers to think in the short term?

If you aren't fired with enthusiasm, you'll be fired with enthusiasm.

-Vince Lombardi

350.

Prepare a speech about your work to deliver to a kindergarten class. Think about all the questions the children may ask you. How will you respond?

It usually takes me about three weeks to prepare a good impromptu speech.

-Mark Twain

351. Keep a journal of interesting thoughts and ideas. Refer to it often and build on it.

352. Identify all of the paradoxes related to your work. What opportunities are hidden in these paradoxes?

353. Next time you go to a laundry ask them to rotate the buttons on your shirts and transfer the dirt from one shirt to another.

354. Sleep in very late some morning and focus on your thinking.

355. Read *The Tao of Pooh*.

356. Mix up your senses. Use a sense other than the normal one to take in information about things you experience. For example, how does your favorite song smell? How does your favorite flower feel?

357. Write down some key questions that you have about your life or work, using your normal writing hand. Then write down the answers using your opposite hand.

358. Have a staring contest with your dog or cat.

359. Go cross country skiing.

360. Identify all of the things that you don't understand. Start with things that relate to key opportunities which are confronting you now. Later, work on other areas.

361. Go dancing.

362. Take a vacation and completely forget everything connected to your work.

**363.**

Learn the practice of "soft eyes" in which you concentrate on de-focusing your eyes so that you can bring in the largest visual field available to you.

You can really see a lot by observing.

-Yogi Berra

A great many people think they are thinking, when they are merely rearranging their prejudices.

-William James

364.

Think about all of the idea-killing statements that you have heard (or perhaps said). Turn these into idea-supporting statements.

A vision without a task is but a dream, a task without a vision is drudgery, a vision and a task is the hope of the world.

-1730, A church in Sussex, England

365.

Identify at least 10 different ways that help you to get out of your thinking box. If you wish to have your ideas included in *How to Get Out of Your Thinking Box, Part 2*, please send them to me at the address on the following page. If your ideas are used in the book, you will receive credit.

Send your ideas to:

Lindsay Collier
P.O. Box 352
West Henrietta, New York 14586
Telephone: 716-334-4779
Fax: 716-359-9744

Epilog

Wishing you the best of luck with all of your _creative_ endeavors.

L.C.
May 1994

About The Author

Lindsay Collier is founder and president of Creative Edge Associates, a consulting firm dedicated to helping clients achieve personal transformation and breakthroughs in their work. He is a consultant, popular speaker, workshop leader, and the author of numerous technical reports and articles on creativity, humor, strategic exploration, work system designs, leadership, and future studies. His work was published in the *Wall Street Journal* and other publications. He appeared on NBC Today. One of his forthcoming books is *Creating Breakthrough in Organizations: Beyond The Whack-A-Mole Theory*.

He is the president of the Rochester (NY) Professional Consultants Network; president of the Western New York Futurists (a chapter of the World Future Society); past director and chapter president of the Institute of Industrial Engineers; and technology leader for Creativity, Innovation, and Strategic Exploration at Eastman Kodak Company (for 24 years). He was the originator of Kodak's "humor room". Lindsay was a former associate of Joel Barker's Infinity Limited Institute. He is a member of: International Creativity & Innovation Network; American Society of Training and Development; Organizational Development Network; World Future Society; Noetic Society; International Speaker's Network; and Creative Education Foundation.

Married with three grown children, Lindsay now lives in West Henrietta, New York.

(OK To Photocopy Order Form)

To order additional copies of *Get Out Of Your Thinking Box*, fill out and send the following information. Please help us to control costs by sending payment with all orders. Thank you.
Send me _____ copies at a total cost of $_____.

$7.95 each, plus $2.50 for first book (S&H) and $0.50 each additional copy. Save on larger orders! Order 10 copies for your friends or organization for Only $69.00 (Free shipping!)

Ship books to:

Name:	_____		
Organization:	_____		
Address:	_____		
City:	_____	State: _____	Zip: _____
Telephone:	_____	Fax:	_____

Order books from the publisher:
Robert D. Reed
750 La Playa, Suite 647 • San Francisco, CA 94121 • Telephone: 1-800-PR-GREEN

(OK To Photocopy Order Form)

To order additional copies of *Get Out Of Your Thinking Box*, fill out and send the following information. Please help us to control costs by sending payment with all orders. Thank you. Send me _____ copies at a total cost of $_____.

$7.95 each, plus $2.50 for first book (S&H) and $0.50 each additional copy. Save on larger orders! Order 10 copies for your friends or organization for Only $69.00 (Free shipping!)

Ship books to:

Name: _____

Organization: _____

Address: _____

City: _____   State: _____   Zip: _____

Telephone: _____   Fax: _____

Order books from the publisher:
Robert D. Reed
750 La Playa, Suite 647 • San Francisco, CA 94121 • Telephone: 1-800-PR-GREEN